KT-578-426
The Professor directs the body's defence system. He and Metro, his lieutenant, work to protect your body. Globus and his team of red blood cells need protection as they travel the body delivering oxygen. So Captain Courageous, chief of the white corpuscles and his friends Ace and Corpo cruise around the body attacking their enemies Virulus, the virus and Toxicus, the bacterium.
PLASMUS
GLOBINA
GLOBUS
VIRULUS

CONTENTS

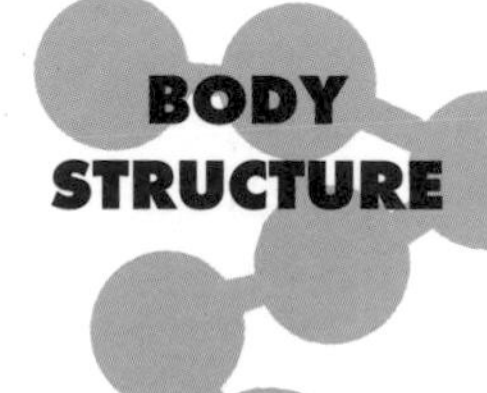

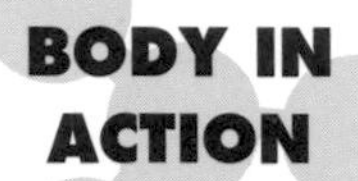

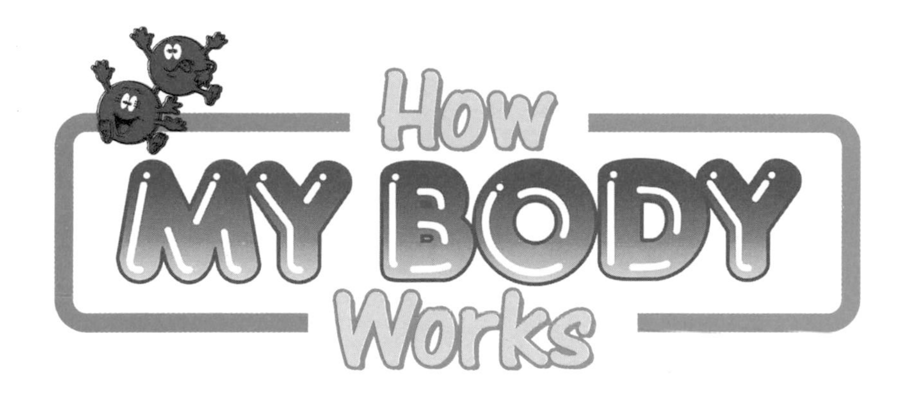

Circulation

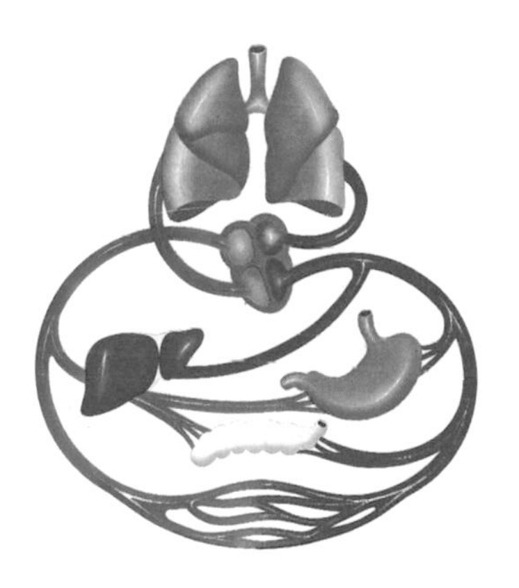

Keep On Pumping

The body's engine

A healthy person is not really aware of having a heart, or of the important work it does in making the body work properly. The heart is the strongest organ in the body, and it works like a pump. Just imagine the amount of work it has to do every day of your life to make sure that the blood reaches every part of your body.

But even the healthiest heart will weaken with time. The heart is like an engine which can wear out and break down completely. If it does, we are in trouble, since there is then nothing to pump the blood – which contains vital oxygen and nutrients (food substances) – around the body.

In the Western world, heart problems are the most common cause of death. That is why it is so important to look after your heart now so that there is less chance of suffering from heart disease when you are older.

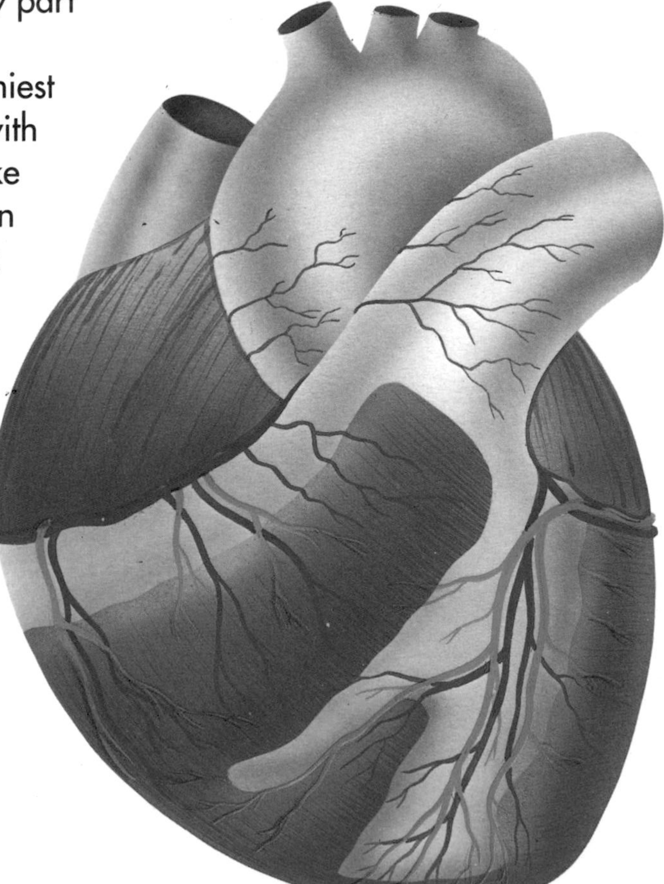

The muscle of the heart is like a machine with a regular beat, similar to a clock. But like any other mechanism, the heart can lose its rhythm. If it does, cardiologists, or heart specialists, are the 'mechanics' who can put the heart back into working order.

This little boy loves spending time with his grandfather, who is still fit and well in his old age. He has obviously looked after his heart, avoiding all the things that are bad for it.

Make sure that you do not become overweight, and that you do not eat too much fatty food and sugar. Smoking is bad for the heart as well as for the rest of your body. The best thing to do is to take lots of exercise and eat healthy foods. Then you can keep the right weight for your age and height, and improve the performance of your heart and keep it healthy for life.

Do you remember?

How blood circulates

The most important task of circulation is to carry oxygen and nutrients to all the tissues in the body. It also removes waste products.

An average adult has five litres of blood. The heart and a very complicated network of blood vessels carry the blood around the body. The blood, carrying carbon dioxide, is pumped from the heart to the lungs, where the carbon dioxide is exchanged for oxygen. The oxygen-rich blood then returns to the heart.

The heart is situated in the middle of the ribcage, sloping down slightly to the left, between the two lungs. It is a muscular pump in the chest, and the muscle goes in and out (contracts and relaxes) in a set rhythm. The heart is hollow inside and has a right half and a left half. Each of these halves is further divided into the atrium (top) and the ventricle (bottom).

The left side pumps the blood with oxygen out of the lungs and distributes it to the rest of the body (this is the **systemic circulation**). The right side pumps blood carrying carbon dioxide into the lungs, where it picks up oxygen again before returning to the heart (this is the **pulmonary circulation**).

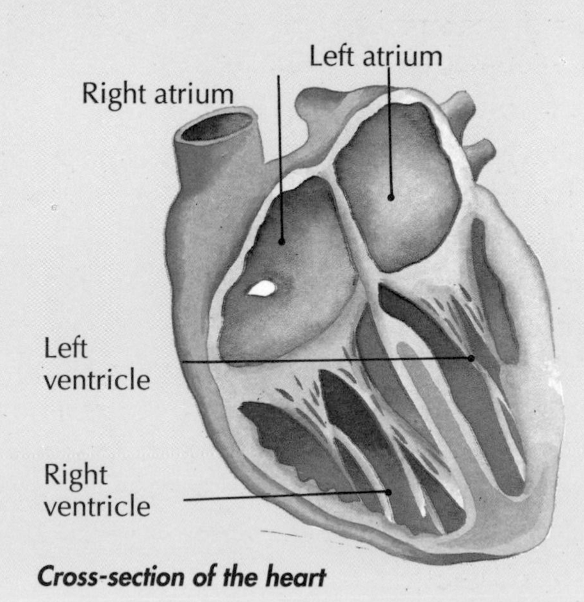

Cross-section of the heart

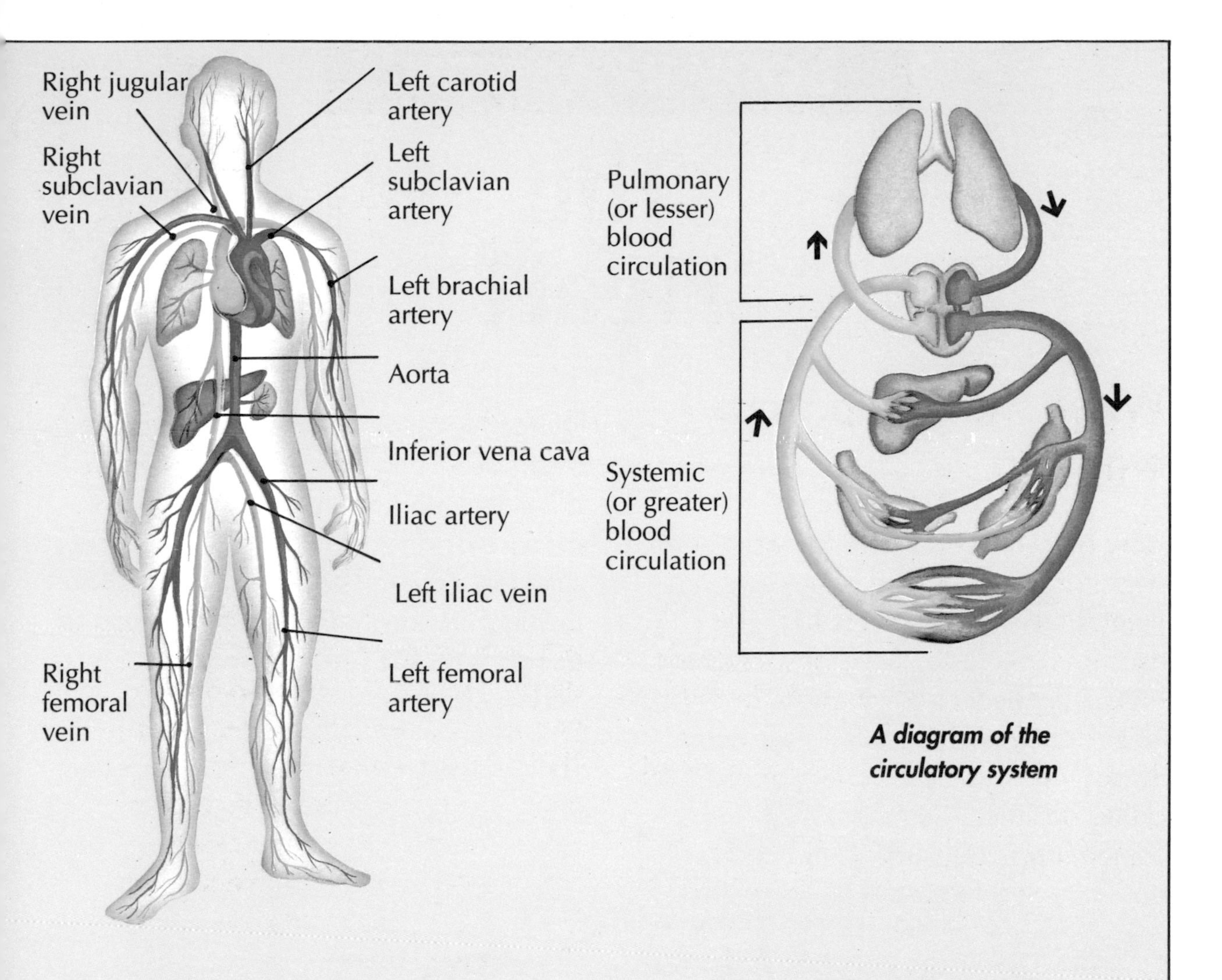

A diagram of the circulatory system

As you can see in the diagram (above right), the blood in the body always flows in the same direction. Arteries take blood with carbon dioxide out of the heart and veins bring the blood back, with oxygen. It takes about 45 seconds for blood to circulate round the body through the millions of blood vessels, which would circle the world twice if they were placed end to end.

Blood travels from the heart through the arteries (marked in red on the diagrams), which have strong, elastic walls to stand up to the pressure constantly put on them by the flow of blood. The arteries branch out further and further until they finally reach the capillaries in the cells.

The capillaries join up to form veins (marked in blue), which carry the blood back to the heart. Veins have thinner walls than arteries, and have valves to prevent the blood from flowing backwards. All these things – the heart, the arteries, the veins and the capillaries – make up the **circulatory system**.

The Heart

When the pump stops working

How hard and how fast the heart beats depends on what kind of physical or mental activity you are doing – for example, exercise, stress or excitement makes the heart beat strongly, or throb. This is quite normal, but if your heart throbs when you are resting or just going upstairs, then there might be something wrong with your heart and you may need to see a doctor.

Other symptoms that show something might be wrong with your heart are difficulty with breathing, reddening of the face or dizziness. Too much alcohol, smoking, tea and coffee can also cause the heart to throb. It can also happen to people who are feverish or to very nervous people.

After strenuous exercise, your heart will beat harder and faster. This is quite normal, and the throbbing should stop after you have rested for a while. If it doesn't, there might be a problem with your heart.

Many healthy people sometimes feel stabbing pains around the heart, but there is usually nothing to worry about. There is a simple remedy – taking long, slow breaths, in and out. These pains are normally due to nerves and the very complicated way our body works.

Sometimes the heart can miss a beat. This happens when the heart muscle contracts before it should and stumbles over a beat, and there is a longer period before the next beat. This causes an unpleasant sensation, but there is no need to be alarmed by it.

The Professor is telling this young boy about the heart and how important it is to look after it.

Cardiac arrest and its causes

When the heart muscle stops pumping completely, this is called a **cardiac arrest**. The most common cause is myocardial infarction (heart attack), which may result in death. But recently doctors have been able to make the heart beat again by heart massage. They can do this as long as they reach the patient very soon after the heart has stopped beating.

It would be more accurate to talk of a 'cardiac-blood' circulation arrest than just 'cardiac' arrest because it is not just the heart but also the blood which stops circulating during a cardiac arrest. When this happens the blood can no longer carry oxygen, which is needed by all the tissues in the body.

Every heart will stop beating at some point, because every living being must eventually die. When the heart is overstrained, it does not have enough strength to contract properly. This means

It is very unlikely that a young child has a heart attack. But if you do see someone having a heart attack, call a doctor or an ambulance immediately.

Even if the heart has already stopped beating there is a short period during which it is still possible to revive the person through heart massage.

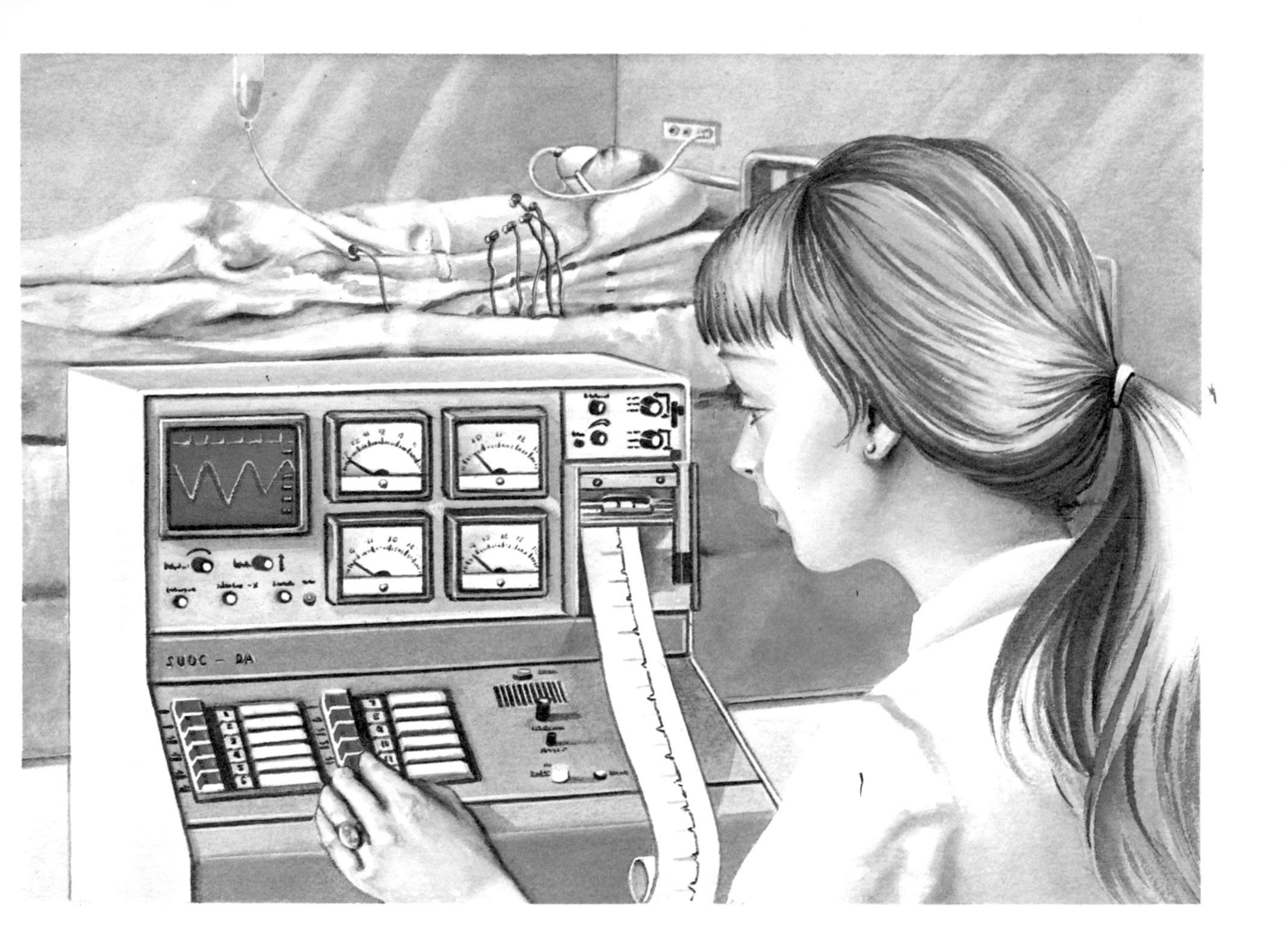

that it cannot pump out all the blood it contains, and extra blood left in the heart slowly increases the pressure on its walls and stops the blood from circulating normally. The heart becomes more and more exhausted until it finally stops working.

Cardiac arrest can also be caused by a lack of oxygen in the blood. Because it works so hard, the heart needs a lot of oxygen. Enough oxygen is therefore vital for the smooth running of the heart. If there is a lack of oxygen, or **anoxia**, the heart will stop beating.

If the heart attack victim reaches hospital in time, there is a very good chance that the doctors will make the heart work again. Hospitals have special coronary care units with highly experienced heart specialists and very advanced equipment to treat heart diseases.

Who is at risk?

How likely someone is to have a heart attack depends on a number of things.

- **Smoking**: This is one of the greatest dangers. A heavy smoker (anyone smoking over 15 cigarettes a day) is considered at risk.
- **Diet**: Foods rich in fats such as bacon, butter and eggs can affect the blood circulation because they create high levels of cholesterol (a white, crystal-like substance) in the blood. Too much cholesterol leads to **atherosclerosis** (a build-up of fatty deposits on the lining of the arteries) which can cause heart disease. Being overweight also puts you in danger.
- **Higher than normal blood pressure**, or **hypertension**: This has a direct effect on heart disease, especially in young people.
- **Hereditary reasons** (passed on through genes from one generation to another): The risk of heart disease increases when a close relative (parents or grandparents) suffer or have suffered from heart disease. If there has been no case of severe heart disease in your family, you are less likely to have a heart attack yourself.
- **Emotional stress**: Constant worry, anxiety and stress are among the chief causes of heart disease.

All these things increases the risk of heart disease. The part played by each one depends on individual cases. Treatment will only be successful if the patient gives up all harmful habits, whether the disease is caused by physical problems (high blood pressure), worrying, or bad living habits (unhealthy diet, smoking and alcohol).

Hereditary reasons

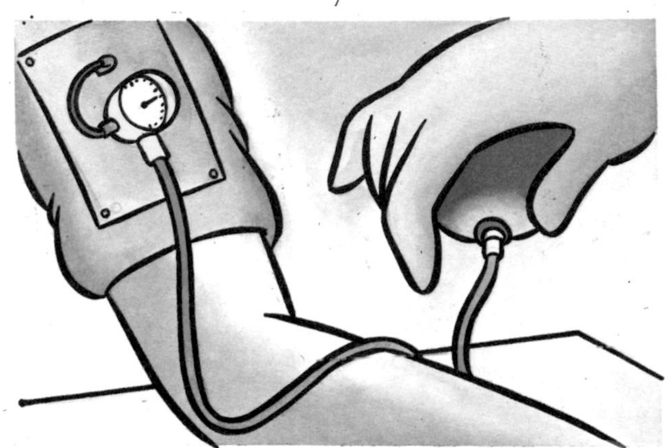

High blood pressure

Bad living habits

Causes of heart disease

Areas affected by angina pectoris

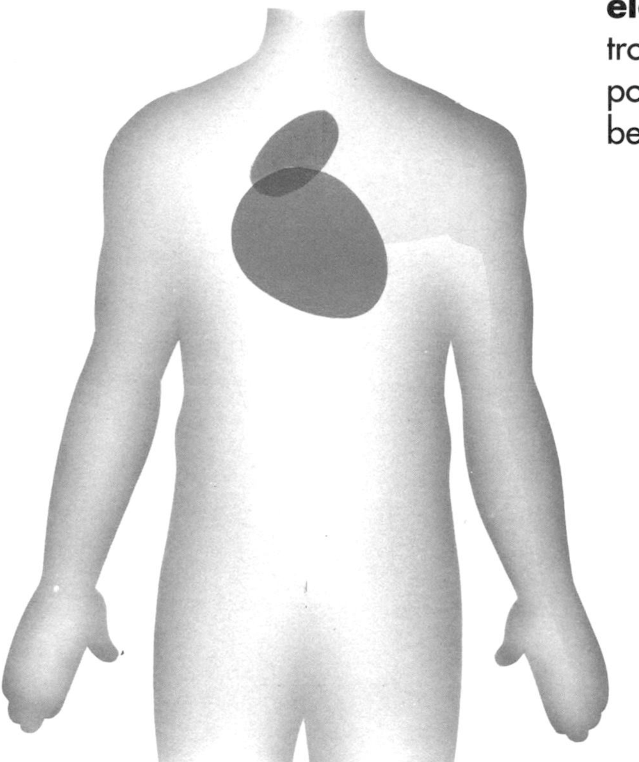

A doctor can diagnose heart disease by using an instrument called an **electrocardiograph** (**ECG**). Heart trouble must be investigated as soon as possible in order to be able to treat it before it becomes fatal (cause death).

Common heart diseases

Angina pectoris and myocardial infarction are two of the commonest diseases in the Western world. **Angina pectoris** is the term used to describe the pain caused when the vessels are not carrying enough blood to the heart muscle. The pain occurs especially during hard physical exercise, because during this the heart muscle needs much more blood.

The pain starts in the middle of the chest and spreads to the left shoulder, arm and the lower jaw. It's a sharp, deep pain that goes away after a rest.

In the case of **myocardial infarction**, part of the heart muscle is destroyed. This causes severe pain in the chest and can lead to immediate death.

Angina pectoris and myocardial infarction are illnesses that hardly ever affect children and young people. That is why you should not worry about it now. Still, you should be aware of the dangers and get into healthy habits so that you can enjoy a healthy life well into your old age.

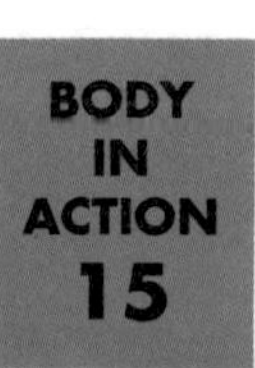

Do you know the normal weight for your age and height? Perhaps your doctor has already told you. Being the correct weight for your height is very important for your health. Eat the right foods and take enough exercise so that you will be less likely to have health problems.

Preventing heart disease

All heart diseases are very difficult to cure, which is why it is much better to try and prevent them. Below, you will find some guidelines which will help fight heart disease.

- **No smoking**: The risk of heart disease is twice as high in a smoker. It's best not to start smoking in the first place, because once you start, it is very difficult to give up.

- **A low-fat diet**: It is best to eat only as much as the body needs and to have light meals. You should avoid food cooked in animal fats as much as possible and eat only one egg a day at the most. Too much milk and bacon is also bad for you. Don't use too much butter or lard in cooking – vegetable oil is much better for you. Get to like eating fish, poultry, fruit and vegetables.

- **Don't be overweight**: People who are overweight run a greater risk than others of suffering from heart disease. You will be overweight if you get into bad eating habits and eat too much and don't take enough exercise. If someone is so overweight, or obese, that it becomes dangerous to the health, a doctor can recommend a special diet to lose weight. If you start eating the right things when you are young, it is easier to keep eating healthy foods when you are older.

- **Avoid emotional stress or anxiety**: These are very common causes of angina pectoris or coronary thrombosis. If you are anxious about a problem at school or at home, work out why it worries you and try to solve it if possible. If you are in a stressful situation which you cannot avoid, such as taking exams, playing sport is an excellent way to forget about them. A good night's sleep is also very important for the body and mind so that you feel rested and well for the following day.

Blood circulation in the heart

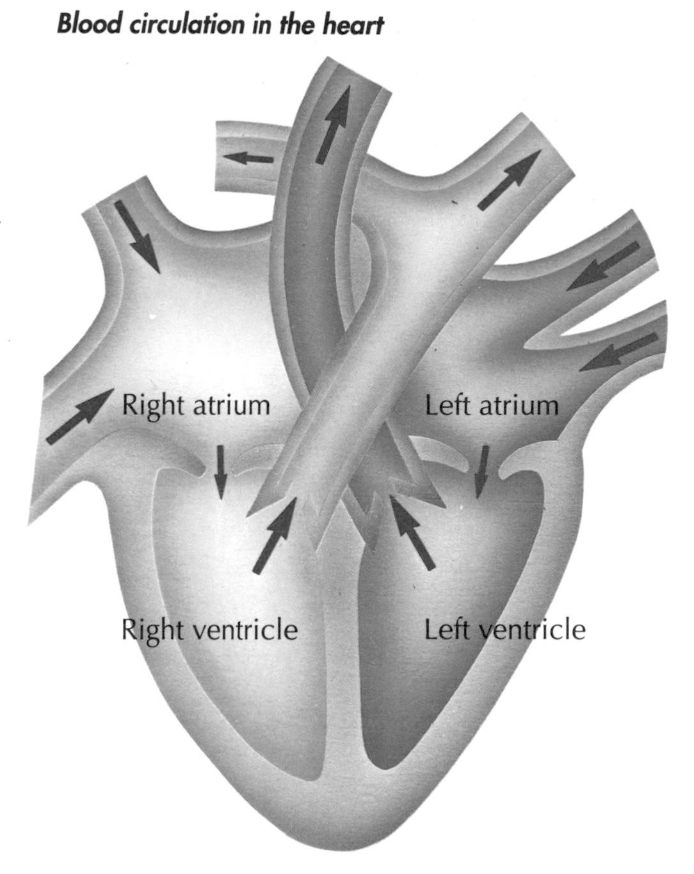

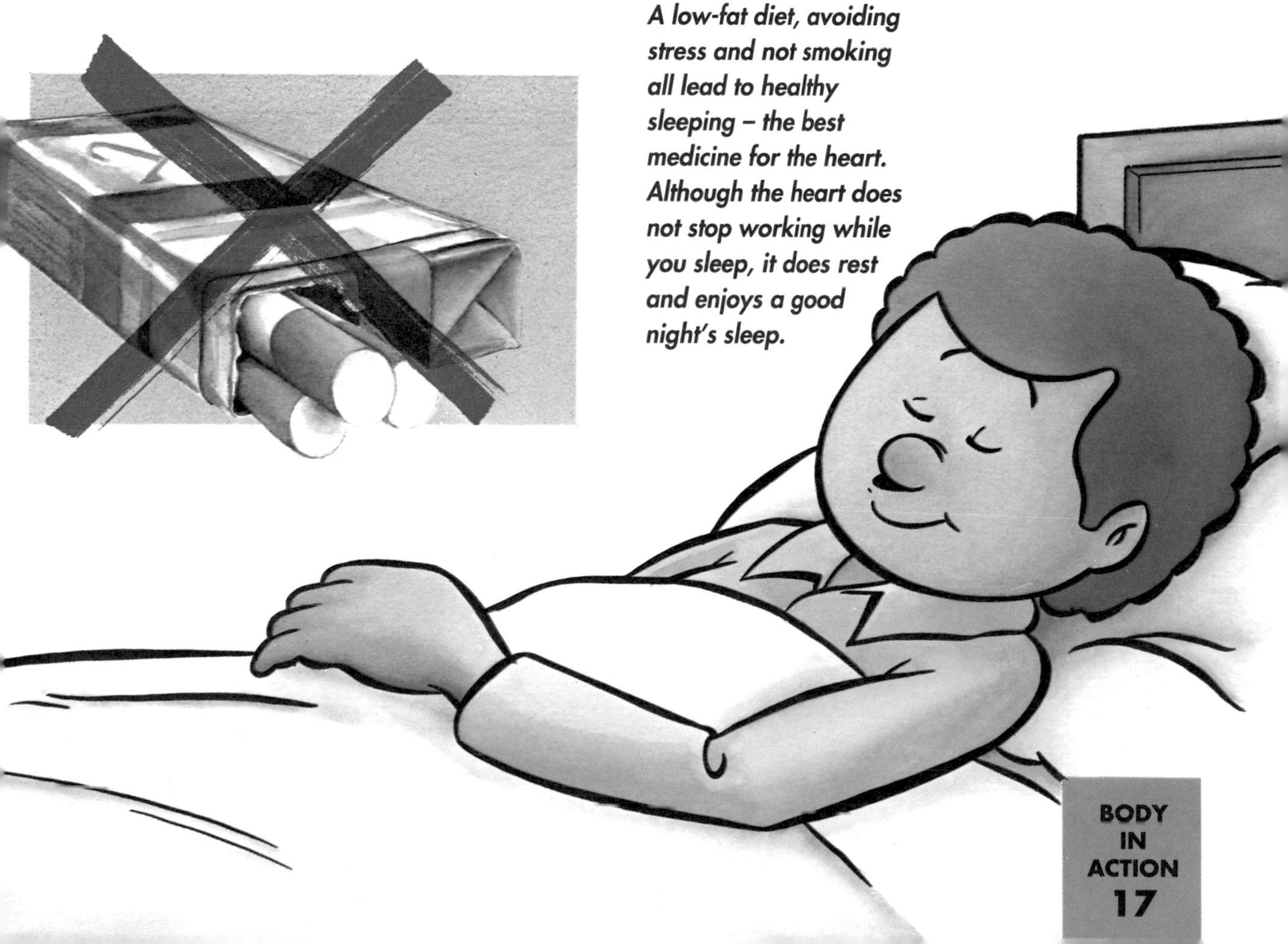

A low-fat diet, avoiding stress and not smoking all lead to healthy sleeping – the best medicine for the heart. Although the heart does not stop working while you sleep, it does rest and enjoys a good night's sleep.

Is your blood pressure normal?

Blood pressure is very important because it gives an accurate picture of how well the heart and the blood vessels are working. It is measured by the pressure caused by the flow of blood through the main arteries. Blood pressure rises and falls depending on how hard the heart muscle has to work – for instance, blood pressure is higher after strenuous exercise and lower when resting or asleep.

The highest blood pressure is measured when the heart muscle contracts and the blood rushes through the aorta, the main artery leaving the heart. This is called **systolic pressure**. During rest, when the heart muscle relaxes, the blood pressure decreases until it reaches its lowest point – **diastolic pressure**.

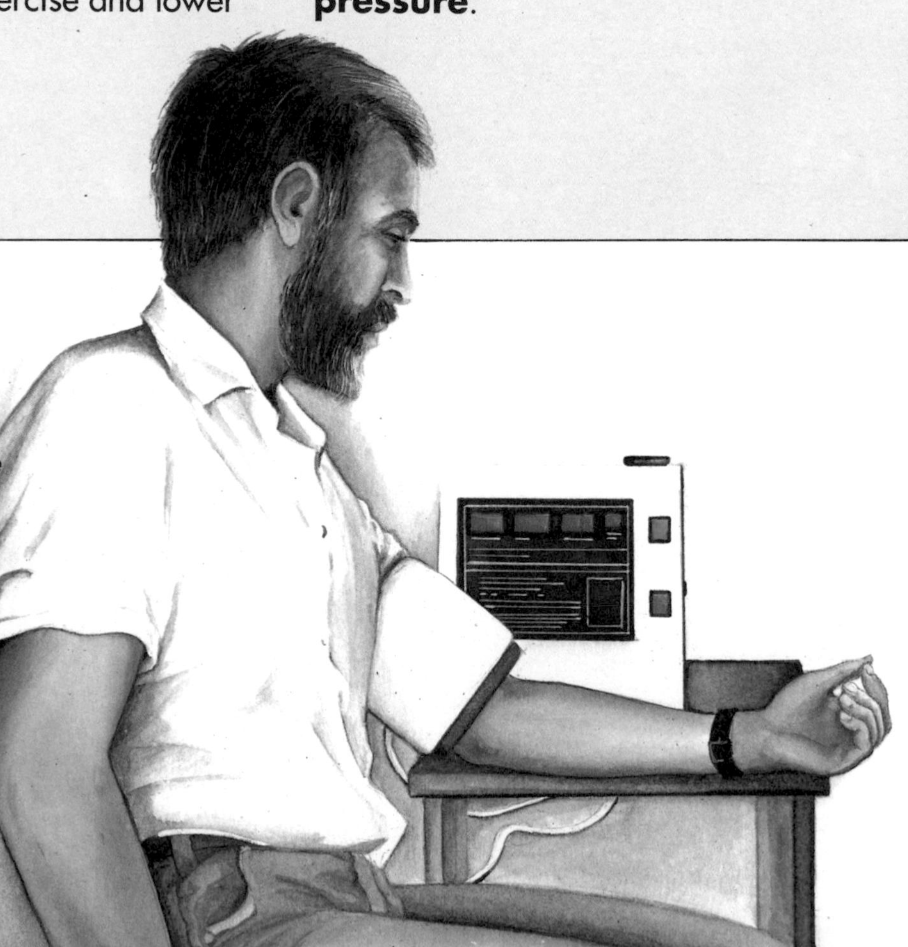

A sphygmomanometer consists of a cuff with an inflatable inside which is wrapped around the upper arm, a rubber bulb to inflate the inside, and a dial that indicates the pressure of blood. Modern sphygmomanometers usually have a spring gauge and dial, or a digital display (as here).

This is an old-fashioned sphygmomanometer with a spring and dial. Earlier instruments used a glass column filled with mercury.

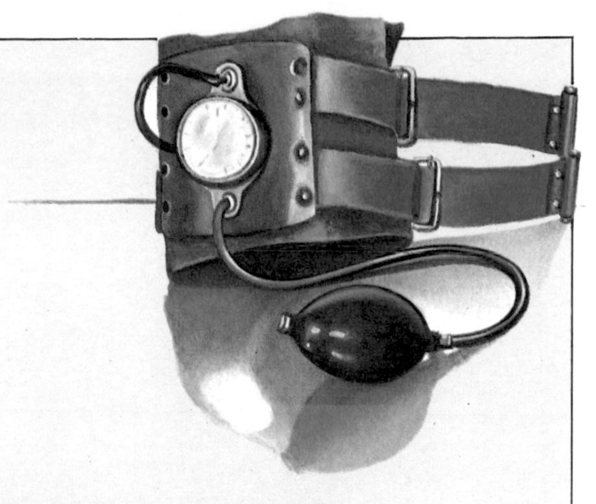

Blood pressure is recorded by giving the systolic pressure and diastolic pressure, and it is measured in millimetres of mercury (mm Hg). Below is a chart of normal blood pressure levels, set by the World Health Organisation. If you have normal blood pressure, the diastolic pressure level should be about half that of the systolic pressure level, plus 10.

Blood pressure tends to rise with age, but not always. Systolic pressures between 110 and 140, and diastolic pressures between 70 and 90 is normal at any age. It is very important for adults to have their blood pressure checked at least once a year. This is done with an instrument called a **sphygmomanometer**.

The medical term given for the condition when blood pressure is higher than it should be is **hypertension**. This can be very dangerous because it could make an artery burst and cause **haemorrhaging** (a medical term for bleeding). If the blood pressure is too low – called **hypotension** – it may cause an arterial disease such as **arteriosclerosis** (thickening or hardening of the arteries).

AGE (years)		SYSTOLIC PRESSURE	DIASTOLIC PRESSURE
CHILDREN			
	3–6	110	70
	6–9	120	75
male	14	132	80
female	14	128	80
ADULTS			
30		130	75
40		140	80
50		150	85
60		160	90/95

This chart shows a sample of blood pressure levels of males and females in different age groups. Blood pressure is always shown with two figures – for example, 130/80 in healthy young people.

A healthy heart

The heart has to work day and night. In order to be able to operate without interruption it needs a constant supply of oxygen-rich blood. The blood vessels make sure that the heart receives enough blood during both physical activity and periods of rest.

Everyone should take regular physical exercise, but it is important to remember not to do too much too suddenly, especially if you are middle-aged or older. The best way to exercise is to start slowly and gently, gradually building up the time and the amount of energy spent on the type of exercise you choose to do. If you are overweight or have a weak heart, it is wise to see your doctor before taking up any kind of sport.

You can avoid many serious illnesses caused by heart or blood circulation disorders by taking gentle physical exercise. The heart will benefit even more if you exercise regularly and eat a healthy, balanced diet, and staying the right weight for your height.

When you take regular exercise, your heart gradually 'learns' to beat more slowly, and therefore more efficiently. A healthy heart gets stronger with regular physical exercise and is then able to pump a larger amount of blood through the blood vessels. After a few months'

Our two friends Globus and little Globina are sitting inside the healthy heart of a fit sportsman, watching the blood flow by steadily. The blood is full of oxygen, which makes sure that the heart muscle works perfectly and never misses a beat.

training, good sportsmen – especially cyclists, swimmers and runners – have a rate of only 50 beats per minute. You see how important physical exercise is for your health – but you must not overdo it!

The heart of a fit sportsman has strong muscle walls. During a hard match, a tennis player's heart will beat more slowly but it will be pumping a larger volume of blood through the blood vessels than the heart of someone who does not exercise regularly.

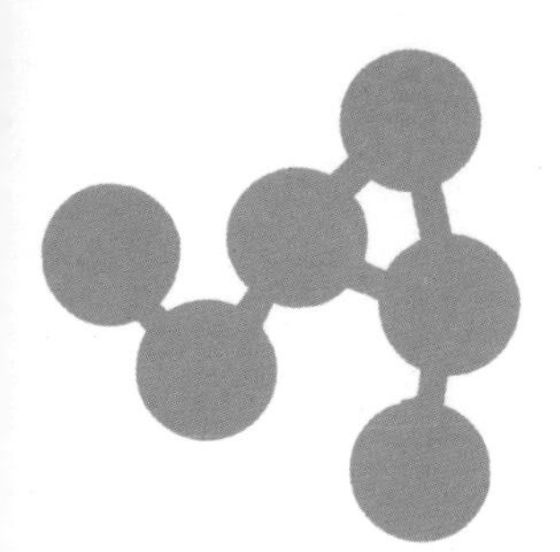

The Blood Vessels

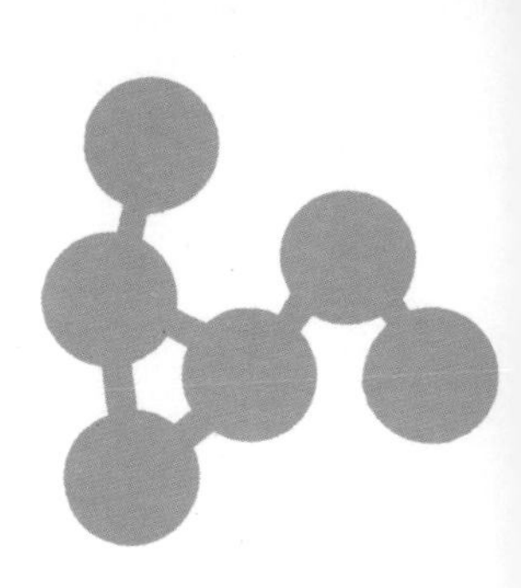

Enemy number one – cholesterol

Like every other part of your body, the arteries get worn down as you get older. The commonest arterial disease is **atherosclerosis**. This is a group of disorders that cause the artery walls to thicken and lose their elasticity. The main cause of artherosclerosis is a fatty substance called **cholesterol**, which is both taken in through food and produced by the liver. Cholesterol is deposited on the artery walls and causes hardening and loss of elasticity.

When the level of cholesterol in the blood rises, lumps collect on the artery walls and begin to block blood flow. Anyone suffering from atherosclerosis must have regular check-ups. These include:

- checking blood pressure
- checking the blood for fat content
- checking body weight, because excess weight is one of the causes of high blood pressure and high cholesterol levels in the blood.

No doubt you will have heard the word 'cholesterol' mentioned by adults in conversation. This is a fatty substance which many grown-ups worry about with good reason.

A high cholesterol level in the blood causes many problems in the blood circulation. On the left is a molecule of cholesterol, which is mostly made by the liver from various foods but is also present in eggs and dairy products. It is an important part of the body cells but too much of it can be very dangerous for the body.

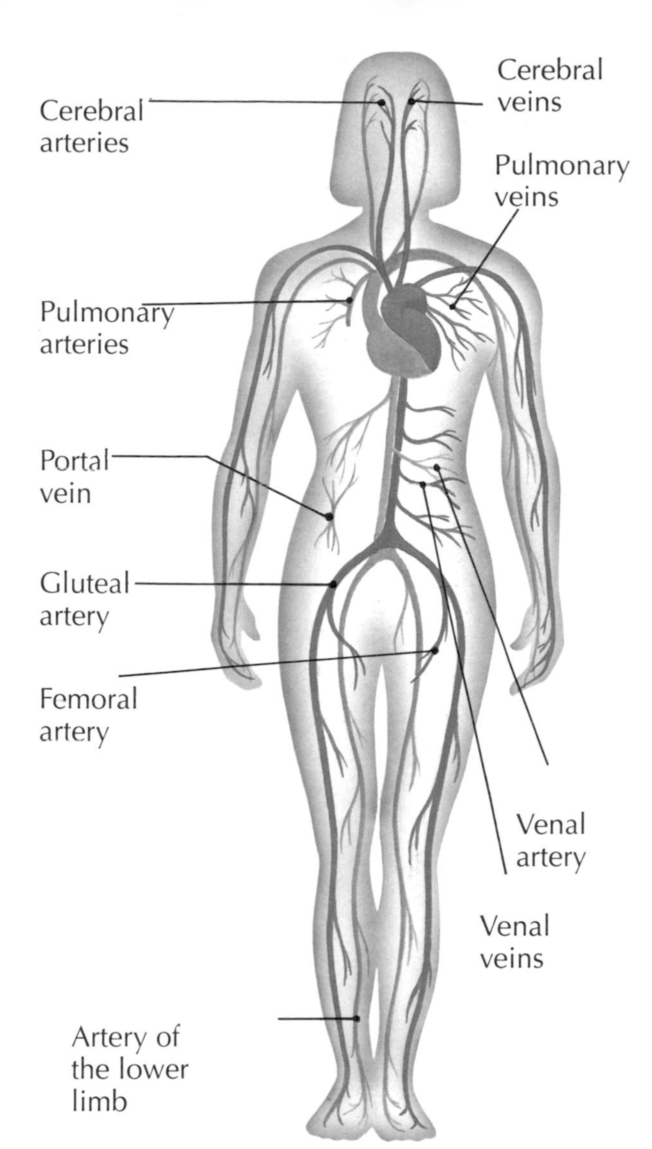

Arterial diseases are most common in the blood vessels of the brain, lungs and heart.

REASONS FOR A HIGH LEVEL OF CHOLESTEROL

- unhealthy diet
- smoking
- high blood pressure
- diabetes
- being over-weight
- lack of exercise
- uric acid in the blood
- hereditary reasons
- heart trouble

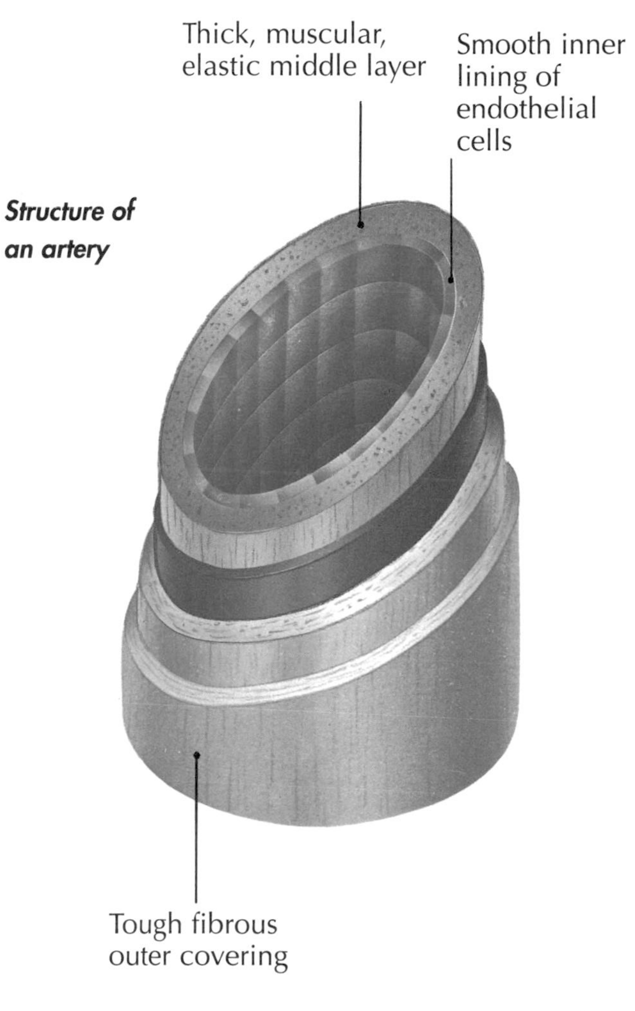

Structure of an artery

What is a stroke?

Twenty percent of the blood which circulates in your body is used by the brain, so you can imagine how hard the brain arteries have to work. A constant supply of oxygen and glucose – substances which are vital to the brain – is carried through these arteries. If one of them became blocked and these vital substances could not reach the brain, brain cells would be destroyed. This is called a **stroke** and it can lead to death or paralysis (loss of movement).

People who suffer from atherosclerosis, high blood pressure or diabetes are most at risk. Smoking also increases the risk of having a stroke. It is possible for the patient to recover fully from a light stroke but more serious strokes can be fatal.

Too much pressure can cause an artery to burst like a balloon which has been blown up too much. **Thrombosis** is the formation of a blood clot anywhere in the blood circulatory system, while an **embolism** is a 'wandering' blood clot which blocks up a blood vessel.

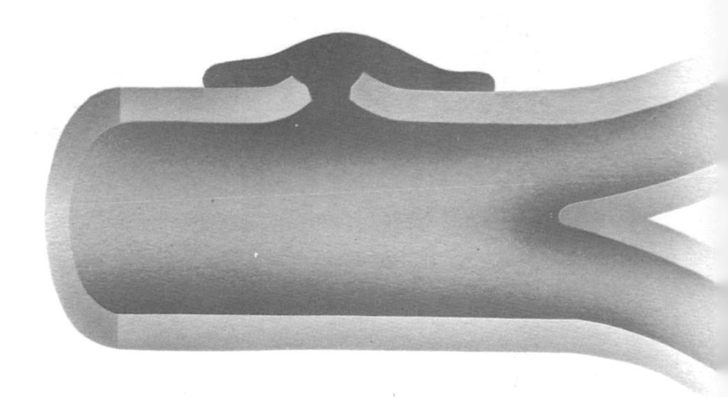

Haemorrhage

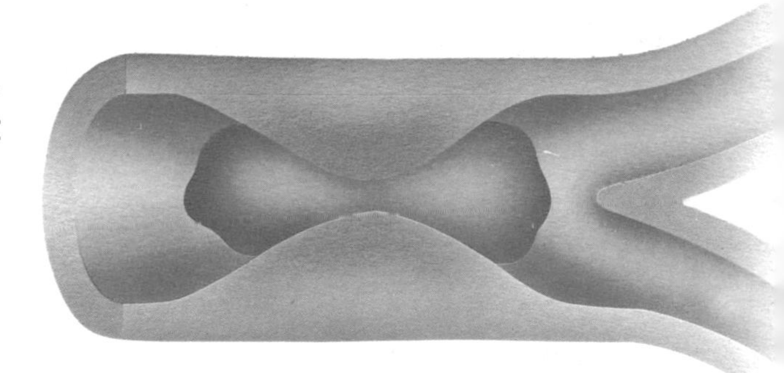

Thrombosis

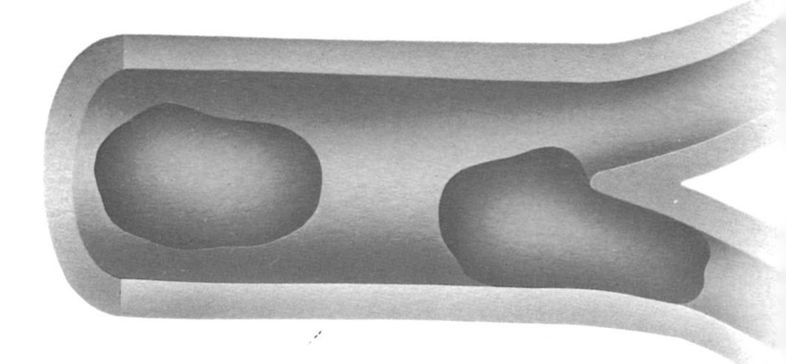

Embolism

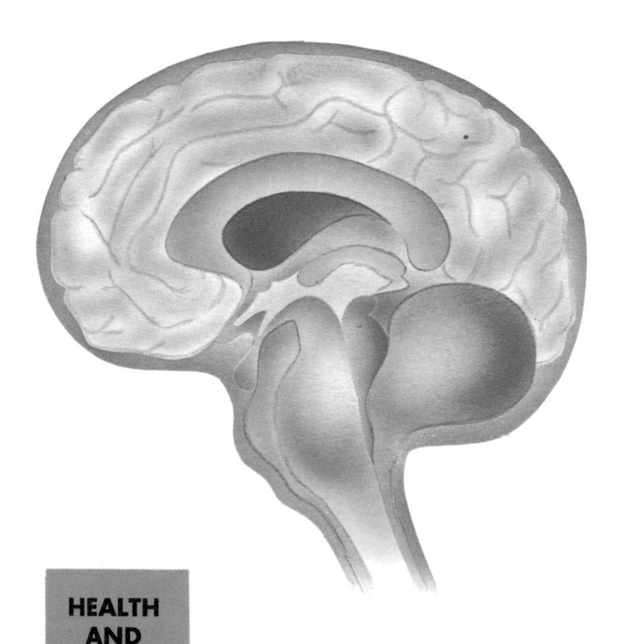

The brain needs a constant supply of blood for it to work properly. A stroke, or apoplexy, can be caused by a brain haemorrhage, or by a blockage of the blood vessels in the brain as a result of embolism or thrombosis.

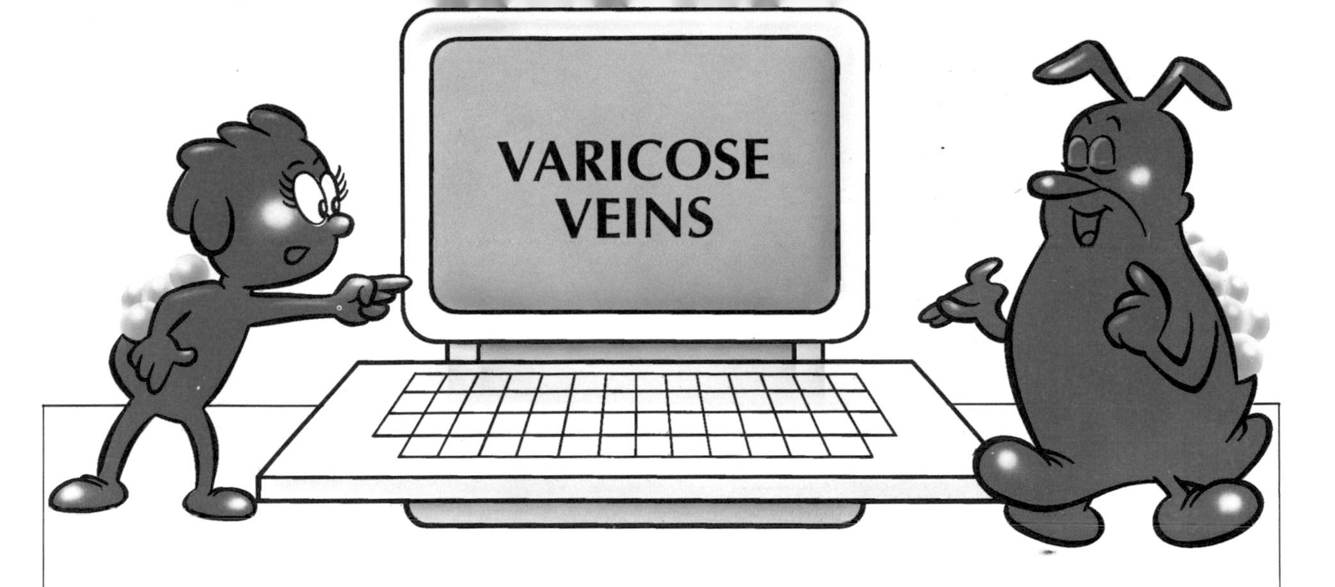

Varicose veins are enlarged or twisted veins just under the skin. They can be very irritating and painful, but they are not fatal. Most common on the legs, varicose veins can be hereditary, or they can appear if you are very overweight. In women they can also be caused by hormonal changes and pressure on the pelvic veins during pregnancy. They may also appear if you have a job where you stand up for long periods of time.

Usually, the blood circulates smoothly through the leg veins, helped by vein valves and leg muscles. Varicose veins occur when there is a blockage in the system and the circulation of the blood becomes sluggish. Anyone suffering from varicose veins must sit with their feet up several times a day. This makes sure that the blood circulates more easily – something which was not previously happening properly as result of weakened veins, valves and blood vessels. There are various ways to treat varicose veins – with drugs and by being more active. In serious cases doctors can operate on them.

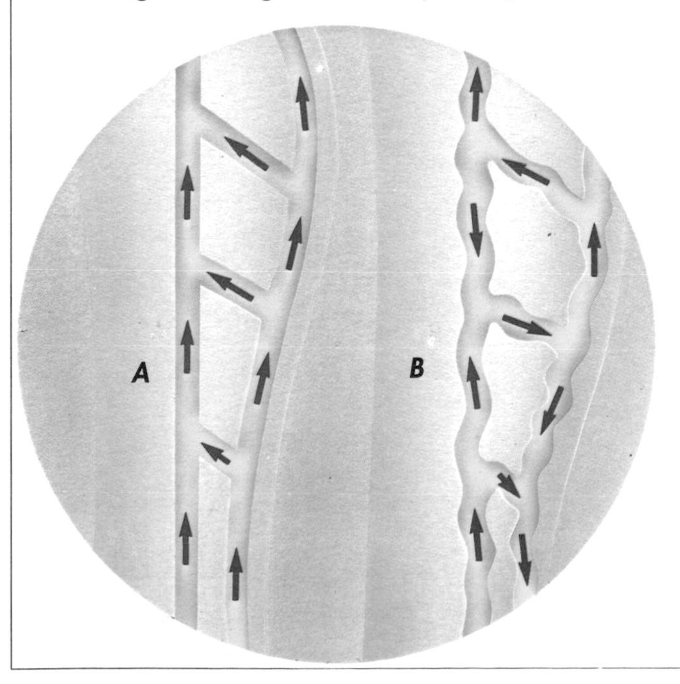

Varicose veins are extremely common, affecting about 10-15 per cent of adults, most of whom are women.
A. Healthy veins
B. Twisted and swollen varicose veins

KEEP MOVING

Get in the right gear

If you are going to take up a sport to become more healthy, make sure that you have the right clothes. Every type of sport needs its own special type of clothing. It is important for sports clothes to be practical rather than fashionable. They must let air through and keep a balanced temperature but still allow complete freedom of movement.

There is a big difference between the clothes for summer sports and winter sports. Summer sports clothes must allow you to perspire, because if your body is unable to control its temperature through sweating, some physical exertion could raise your body temperature to a life-endangering 42 degrees. That is why

Clothes worn by athletes should allow complete freedom of movement as well as perspiration. Light clothes with shorts are worn for many types of sport.

Every sporting activity requires suitable clothes which keep the body temperature at a constant level.

summer sports clothes should be loose and light.

Cold weather clothes must prevent the loss of body heat. The parts of the body which are particularly sensitive to cold should be specially protected. These parts are the ears, neck, lower part of the abdomen, hands, ankles and toes. Layers of clothes made from natural fibres and some artificial fibres are best for sports such as skiing and mountaineering.

Above all winter sports clothes must protect the body against the cold, but they should also allow ventilation.

KEY WORDS

Anoxia – a condition when body tissues are without oxygen.
Artery – a tube or vessel that carries blood from the heart.
Atherosclerosis – a build-up of fatty deposits on the lining of the arteries, which can cause heart disease.
Cardiologist – a doctor who specialises in diseases of the heart.
Cholesterol – a white, crystal-like alcohol substance which collects on the artery walls and thought to be the cause of athrosclerosis. It is both taken through food and produced by the liver.
Coronary care unit – a special unit of a hospital that deals with heart problems.
Electrocardiograph – an instrument to measure the heart beat to see if there is anything wrong with the heart.
Embolism – a 'wandering' blood clot which blocks up a blood vessel.
Haemorrhage – a medical term for bleeding.
Hypertension – a condition when the blood pressure is higher than it should be.
Hypotension – when blood pressure is lower that it should be.
Nutrients – food substances that are good for the body.
Thrombosis – clotting in a blood vessel.

HOW MY BODY WORKS

HOW MY BODY WORKS is an educational series that builds into a complete encyclopedia of the human body. Each volume introduces and explains one of its mysteries.

In Part 31 of How My Body Works, you've seen how the blood circulates around the body.

Part 32 takes a close look at the lungs and breathing, and all the illnesses that affect our breathing system.

READ ALL ABOUT:

- **What air pollution does** to our lungs.
- **Dangerous diseases** of the respiratory system.
- **How you can help** prevent some of these diseases.

Albert Barillé (pictured left) is the author of this fascinating series of books. The human body is a series of complex systems and mechanisms, so to make it easier for you to understand how the body works, Barillé created The Professor, Captain Courageous, Globus, Toxicus and Virulus, plus many other colourful cartoon characters, to show you around. The Professor and his friends guide you through the body, explaining how it works in a clear and simple way that makes it fun.

TEST YOUR KNOWLEDGE

The Circulation quiz

More than one answer may be correct

1. How can you improve the performance of your heart?
a) by smoking, drinking and being fat
b) by taking lots of exercise
c) by eating sensibly and keeping the right body weight for your age and height

2. What do cardiologists do?
a) they are health experts
b) they are doctors who specialise in diseases of the heart
c) they are doctors who specialise in diseases of the lungs

3. How much blood does an average adult have in the body?
a) 3 litres
b) 5 litres
c) 7 litres

4. How does blood travel around the body?
a) through the veins
b) through the arteries
c) through the capillaries

5. What is a sphygmomanometer?
a) an instrument that is used to diagnose heart disease
b) an instrument to measure blood pressure
c) an instrument that tells you how much blood there is in the body

6. Why is measuring your blood pressure so important?
a) because it can tell you how well your circulation is working
b) because it can tell you how much you weigh
c) because it can tell you if you have a cold

7. When does your blood pressure go up?
a) after dinner
b) after strenuous exercise
c) after sitting down for a while

8. Why is cholesterol so dangerous?
a) because it forms deposits on artery walls which stop the blood flowing freely
b) because it causes varicose veins
c) because it makes the blood vessels burst

9. Arterial diseases are most common in the blood vessels of:
a) the brain
b) the lungs
c) the heart

10. A blockage in the brain arteries leads to:
a) destruction of brain cells
b) paralysis
c) a stroke

ANSWERS to the '**How My Body Works**' Circulation quiz are in Issue 32.

Answers to Issue 30

1 (b & c), 2 (a), 3 (a, b & c), 4 (b), 5 (c), 6 (c), 7 (a), 8 (c), 9 (a & c), 10 (c), 11 (a, b & c)

Published by
ORBIS PUBLISHING,
Griffin House,
161 Hammersmith Road,
London W6 8SD

BACK ISSUES
Back issues can be obtained by placing an order with your newsagent or, in case of difficulty, from our back numbers department. All cheques/postal orders should be made payable to Orbis Publishing Ltd.

BACK ISSUE CHARGES
Volume 1:
UK: 99p plus £1.00 p&p;
Eire: IR£0.99 plus £1.00 p&p
Thereafter:
UK: £2.99 plus 50p p&p;
Eire: IR£3.50 plus 50p p&p

ADDRESS FOR BACK ISSUES:
Orbis Publishing Ltd, Unit 10, Wheel Lane Business Park, Wheel Lane, Westfield, Hastings, East Sussex, TN35 4SG. Tel: 0424 755755

BACK ISSUES OVERSEAS
Please place requests for copies of back issues with your newsagent or, in case of difficulty, please write to the relevant address given:

Australia
Gordon and Gotch Ltd, PO Box 290, Burwood VIC 3125 (Enclose cover price plus $1 p&h per issue)

New Zealand
Gordon and Gotch (NZ) Ltd, PO Box 584, Auckland.

South Africa
Back issues Dept
Republican News Agency
PO Box 16034
Doornfontein 2028

Malta & Singapore
Back numbers are available at LM1.50 from your newsagent.

N 31 93 11 11
Printed in Italy
by Officine Grafiche
De Agostini, Novara

CAPTAIN COURAGEOUS
METRO
ACE
CORPO
TOXICUS
GERMUS